MASKS
Stories from a Pandemic

Peter Cherches

BAMBOO
DART
PRESS

LOS ANGELES   †   NEW YORK   †   LONDON   †   MELBOURNE

Masks: Stories from a Pandemic by Peter Cherches

ISBN: 978-1-947240-39-1

eISBN: 978-1-947240-40-7

Cover art by Dennis Callaci

Layout and design by Mark Givens

Author photo by Allan Bealy

For information:

Bamboo Dart Press

chapbooks@bamboodartpress.com

Bamboo Dart Press 017

www.pelekinesis.com

www.bamboodartpress.com

www.shrimperrecords.com

In memory of Don Skiles

Grateful acknowledgment is made to the following publications in which these stories first appeared: *Danse Macabre, Flash Boulevard, Love in the Time of COVID*, and *Shift: A Journal of Literary Oddities.*

Contents

Back to School

In my dream I was back in third grade. We were sitting at our wooden desks, with now-vestigial inkwells and palimpsests of graffiti from various years past, such as names and hearts and "Rocco loves Angie" and the occasional crudely drawn cock and balls, etched into the wood with pen knives, all of us wearing masks over our noses and mouths in response to the great pandemic of 1965. Miss Valentine, who would soon become Mrs. Day, stood in front of the class, telling us about all the great advances in immunology in recent years. Then she stopped and aimed her remarks at a kid in the back row, Scot, whom we all called Scot the Snot, not because he acted snotty, but because he had a perennially runny nose as well as congealed mucus encrusting his nostrils. "Scot Merkin!" she shouted. "Where's your mask."

In a quivering voice, on the verge of tears, he said, "I'm sorry, Miss Valentine, but my mask has snot all over it."

"Well," she said, "you'll just have to get another mask. And don't say 'snot,' that's vulgar; say 'mucus.'"

"But every time I put a new mask on it gets full of snot, um, mucus."

"Well, we can't have you sitting here without a mask. Go to the nurse for the time being and we'll see what we can do."

Scot left the room in tears.

Then Johnny Involtini, one of the tough boys, both of whose parents had voted for Goldwater, took off his mask.

"What are you doing, Johnny?" Miss Valentine gasped.

"I got snot too," he said. "I ain't wearin' no stupid mask."

"I'm not wearing any stupid mask," she corrected, just before I woke up with a runny nose.

At the Supermarket

I went to the supermarket on Friday morning, my usual day. Ever since the lockdown started, I've been doing my grocery shopping on Fridays, because that's when they get their weekly delivery of my favorite bread from an upstate artisanal baker. I try to minimize my supermarket visits, as I'd always found them anxiety-provoking, even in normal times. When I work in an office I don't keep much food in the house because I usually go out for lunch and do takeout when I get home. So stocking up on groceries was a novel concept for me, since I'd usually just dash into smaller shops for things I need here and there.

That changed in March, of course. I'd don my face mask and go out on a Friday morning at around 10am. Once I tried 8:30 but they hadn't yet received the bread delivery. In the past I'd just pick up one of those red baskets, more than sufficient for my usual needs, but now I wheel around a full-size cart, which, for some reason, I find anxiety-provoking in itself.

Anyway, this past Friday I was at my local Key Food, mask on, reading glasses atop my head in case I needed to read a label, rolling my cart through the aisle for soup, rice, and pasta, looking for Progresso Chickarina soup, one of the comfort foods of my often miserable childhood, when I saw a little kid, maybe ten years old, perusing the Progresso display. He had a mask on, but from his eyes, hair color, and head shape, I could tell enough to be surprised and a bit frightened. The kid looked just like me as a ten-year-old.

The kid saw me, and I think he smiled—that is, I saw the corners of his eyes crinkle in a way that suggested smiling. Then he started singing the Chickarina jingle:

> Chick-chick-Chickarina soup,
> Chick-chick-Chickarina soup,
> It has chicken so nutritious,
> And meatballs so delicious...

His voice sounded eerily familiar. As an adult, I had never thought about what I might have sounded like as a child, but that's what this kid sounded like, I realized. It was really freaking me out.

"What's your name," I asked the kid.

"I don't have a name," he replied.

"No name? Why is that?"

"Because I don't need a name," he said.

Why wouldn't he need a name? "Why don't you need a name," I asked.

No answer.

I went to look into the kid's eyes again, but his eyes were no longer there—nor the rest of his head, for that matter. Floating above his torso was a blue surgical mask. Then I saw and heard something even more disturbing. The mask was kind of bouncing around, and a voice began to sing the jingle again.

Chick-chick-Chickarina soup,
Chick-chick-Chickarina soup,
It has chicken so nutritious,
And meatballs so delicious...

The voice, seemingly coming from the mask, was my voice, my current voice, that is, my adult voice!

If you can't beat 'em, join 'em, I figured, and I started singing along.

Chick-chick-Chickarina soup,
Chick-chick-Chickarina soup,
It has chicken so nutritious,
And meatballs so delicious...

It was kind of cool, albeit disturbing, this duet, the bouncing mask singing in my adult, trained baritone, and me singing with the innocence and purity of a ten-year-old.

It struck me that while the voice coming from the mask was technically much more adept, my own singing voice now had a patina of sadness that seemed at odds with its newfound innocence and purity—a contrast that provided an affecting tension.

With that realization, the mask and the little boy's body disappeared and my voice returned to my trained, adult baritone. But I also noticed a vulnerability that had been largely missing from my singing until then.

I had never imagined that the Chickarina jingle was such a tear-jerker.

Progress

My doorbell rang. "Who is it?" I asked.

"A neighbor."

I recognized the voice. It was the polar bear from down the hall. I put a mask on and opened the door. Damn, he wasn't wearing a mask. I was about to tell him to put a mask on if he wanted to speak to me, but then I realized he just had one of those surgical masks on backwards, so the white side was showing.

I breathed a sigh of relief and fogged up my glasses.

"So, what can I do for you?" I asked.

"Do you have any ice?" he asked. "I'm all out."

"I'm afraid not. I hardly ever use ice cubes. I used to have a manual defrost freezer, and then I always had ice cubes, but when I replaced it with a self-defrosting one the ice in the trays just disappears over time, poof, and now I have two empty trays in the freezer."

"Tell me about it," the polar bear said. "Progress is a bitch."

On the Street

I didn't recognize him with the red paisley bandana covering the bottom half his face and some big-ass sunglasses and a Yankees cap that had seen better days covering the upper half until I heard his voice, slightly muffled. "Ignoring me, eh?"

"Ah, it's you!" I said, adjusting my blue surgical mask.

"Yes, I am me and you are you and we are all together. I recognized you right away. Not your face, of course, your gait, the way you carry yourself." (Was he implying that I wasn't sufficiently attentive to his gait and the way he carries himself?)

"I guess I was lost in my own thoughts," I said. (Why was I trying to justify myself to him?)

"So, my friend, how are you weathering the storm?" he asked.

"As well as can be expected," I replied.

"As well as can be expected!" I could tell this was the start of one of his tirades by the tone of his voice. "As well as can be expected! What can be expected these days? And who are you to tell me that you and you alone are on top of things, anyway, that you and you alone know what can be expected, that you and only you have what it takes to cope with it?"

I knew better than to argue with him. I knew that would only make matters worse, much worse.

"Let's forget it," I said.

"Forget it!" he said. "He wants me to forget it! Who in hell are you to decide whether I should forget anything?" (I wondered which was the more common phrasing, "who *in* hell" or "who *the* hell.")

"Listen, why don't we get together for lunch sometime," I said, in an attempt to change the subject, to calm him down, to placate him.

"Lunch? You think this is a joke?"

"No joke," I said. "I'd love to catch up, but I don't think here on the street outside the park with masks on is the best idea."

"Well, listen to Mister Superiority!" he said. "Not the best idea! You officious little twerp!"

"So what do you say, eh, lunch? Some outdoor place in the neighborhood? Next week?"

"Sure," he said, "pretend I'm not here. Go on as if I'm some Ken doll with no feelings."

I had no idea where he got that Ken doll from. He was hardly a Ken doll, with or without a mask. More like a Wishnik with slightly better-groomed hair.

"Listen," I said, trying to put an end to this nonsense, "I'd better start heading home now. My bladder is tugging at my sleeve, if you know what I mean."

"Boy, do I know what you mean, man," he said, in a more conciliatory tone. "Give me a call later this week and we'll talk about lunch."

Nothing like bladder solidarity, I thought, partially relieved.

At the Post Office

There was a green postcard in my mailbox. It was from the post office, notice of a package in need of a signature. I'd have to go to the P.O. to sign for my item, something I was not looking forward to in these times of caution, masks, and social distancing. I got out one of my flat surgical masks, since I'm saving the N95s for the subway and, if necessary, longer indoor encounters, and left the apartment.

In my zip code there's a small satellite post office not far from my building, two and a half short blocks, but they don't hold packages there, so I'd have to go to the main branch, about a fifteen-minute walk away. I had gone only once this year, early in the lockdown, to mail out some copies of my new book. It was a little anxiety-provoking, but not too bad, and I'd say it was pretty much the same this time. Everybody was wearing masks—postal workers and customers. One person, a small, elderly, salted-caramel-colored woman (gratuitous skin-tone metaphor added for a scintilla of controversy), had a homemade mask that looked like it was sewn from an old Blue Oyster Cult T-shirt. There were markers on the floor, decals of shoes, spaced at 6-foot intervals. It reminded me of those diagrams for dance instruction with schematic drawings of shoe outlines. Didn't the Kramdens have one of those when Carlos was giving mambo lessons?

The biggest problem with the post office was how long it took to serve each customer. I was fifth in line but I waited close to a half hour. First of all, there were only two clerks. Somebody had a bunch of large envelopes, and the clerk was slowly reviewing the address on each, then looking them all up to make sure they were formatted correctly and had the right plus four zip code, which always reminds me of plus fours, which I don't think I've ever worn, the closest I've ever come to golfing being pitch 'n' putt (and, to be honest, I just now had to look up plus fours because I had always conflated them with union suits and those pajamas with feet). But I digress. Each customer took at least ten minutes. Because of the distancing, the line snaked around and out the door. I was glad I arrived early.

My turn finally came. Number 8 on the electric board lit up, and I went to window 8. I handed my green postcard to the clerk through that little tray under the window you slide things through. "Oh, you need to go to the package pickup window for this," she said.

"Where's that?"

"Right at the end."

"There's nobody there," I said.

"Don't you worry," she said. "You just go over and someone will come by."

So I went over and stood by the package pickup window. Thirty seconds or so, and nobody came by. I could see there was a woman working in the back, putting things in and taking things out of pigeonholes. Should I call to her? Try to get her attention? Or would that be breaking post office protocols, post office etiquette. I waited. Maybe another two or three minutes. Finally I called to the lady of the pigeon-holes. "Excuse me," I said, "is anybody working this window?"

"I don't know where she is," the woman said.

"Can you ask? Or take a look?"

"Give me a minute."

About five minutes later she returned. "She'll be right with you."

Another five minutes later a clerk came to the package pickup window. It was the same woman I had spoken to at window number 8.

I was really annoyed. Why the hell couldn't she have helped me the first time around? In the old days I'd have made a stink. Yes, I could be quite combative back in the day. Then I started smoking weed for my insomnia and I mellowed out, lost my appetite for confrontation. Whatever. I handed her the green postcard. "I'll be right back," she said.

"Right back" in post office time is not the same as "right

back" in human time. She must have been gone about ten minutes. I kept craning my neck at the window to see what was happening in the back, but the woman was nowhere in sight.

She finally returned. "Sorry it took so long," she said. "It was misfiled."

Call me a cynic, but I didn't believe her. Misfiled my ass. I'll bet she was shooting the breeze with one of her coworkers, or maybe using the opportunity to take a dump. But what could I do?

"Can I see your ID?" she asked.

I showed her my driver's license, which I only use for ID as I'm so terrified of driving that I've never gotten behind a wheel since the day the examiner congratulated me, "You have met the minimum requirements."

"Your name's Cherches?" she asked.

"Yes," I said.

"Peter?"

"Yes."

She started cracking up.

"What's so funny?" I asked.

"I'm sorry," she said, "they delivered the card to the wrong mailbox. This package is for St. Peter's Church! Is there anything else I can do for you? No? Well, you have a nice day, then."

One of the Family

As I was out for my morning walk, I saw a woman walking her dog outside the park, a Jack Russell. The dog was wearing a mask over its nose and mouth, and it didn't look too happy. Not sad, not depressed, not like one of those Sarah MacLachlan tug-at-your-heartstrings abused dogs on TV, just pissed off. I could see it in the dog's eyes, that quizzical "What the fuck's this thing doing on my face" look. What *was* the thing doing on the dog's face? I've read that there have been rare, isolated cases of pets becoming sick from close contact with their owners, but we're talking really low risk. And outdoors? Was this going too far?

I asked the woman, "Are you concerned that the dog might catch the virus?"

"Not especially," she said. "We just don't want him to feel left out. Jasper is one of the family."

I nodded politely. Then she took a few steps behind me, knelt down, pulled her own mask down, and sniffed my ass.

On the Subway

The other day I took my first subway ride since the outbreak. I'd been working from home in March, in April I was furloughed, and in July I was permanently laid off. I had to go to my now former office to pick up some personal effects before the skeleton maintenance crew discarded them. I was pretty nervous. I'm fine with outdoors, and brief bodega stops for milk or beer with a mask on don't worry me too much, but the subway was a nest of unknowns. A recent article in the *New York Times* about the relative lack of transmission on public transportation didn't really set my mind at ease. I had ordered some N95 masks from a Hasidic surgical supply business in Brooklyn, specifically for the subway, having read that these offered better protection than the blue rectangular accordion-style surgical masks I usually use, a tighter seal and I think better filtration material. When I put one of the N95s on for the first time, I thought the conical shape sticking out from my face made me look like a peccary.

When I got to the subway platform I switched masks, from surgical to N95. If anything could revive my anxiety attacks of yesteryear, this was it. The train arrived and I took a seat. I looked around. The crowd was sparse, mask here, mask there, very good, then, diagonally across from me, I saw a guy with the mask over his mouth but below the nose; I wondered if I should say something; I didn't say anything. I saw an elderly Asian woman with a mask on sitting next to a younger man, no mask, maybe her son. But I was alone on one of those benches for two at the end of the car, and I figured I had enough distance from the scofflaws. I was about to take my Kindle out of my bag when the door between the cars, right next to me, opened, and in walked a disheveled, shirtless, maskless panhandler. I looked down as he passed me mumbling his spiel. Then the train made a stop; a few passengers got off and an unmasked teenager got on, smoking a reefer. He sat down across from me. I got up and moved to the next car. This looked more promising, similarly sparse, and I didn't notice any unmasked passengers.

I sat down, took out my Kindle, and picked up where I had left off in an Icelandic existential crime thriller. Reading with a mask on is a challenge, as my reading glasses keep getting fogged up. A couple of years ago, before my cataract surgeries, I could have held the book right up to my face and read without glasses, I was that myopic, but now I can't read a thing without reading glasses, though $15 ones off the drugstore rack do just fine. Then, just as I was getting back into the story, I heard those dreaded words coming from the center of the car, "Show time!"

Oh no! I thought, they're going to rain on my reading parade. They're going to do those asinine acrobatics to loud hip-hop music blasting from a distorted boom box. No way I can concentrate on my Icelandic existential crime thriller.

I'm not a hip-hop fan. I don't judge it, mind you, I don't say it's not music, or even that it's not good music, it's just not my bag. I'm old school, not to mention old-ish. I love jazz, bossa nova, and classic late-sixties rock, and oh yeah, classic soul, but not hip-hop, and not that stuff they're calling R&B either, which I don't think stands for rhythm and blues, and certainly has nothing to do with La Vern Baker or Louis Jordan and his Tympany Five.

I do love buskers, and I always support the talented ones, but I don't get these "show time" performers—interchange-able groups of teenagers throughout the subway system with the same shtick, swinging from subway poles while the music blasts. I'm always afraid one of them is going to accidentally kick me in the face. That's entertainment? That takes talent? I suppose it takes a little more talent than painting yourself with poisonous silver or gold pigment and standing stock still for hours on end while tourists take their photos with you or try to make you laugh. Do those guys wear Depends? At least they're quiet.

I put my Kindle down and prepared to weather the "show time" storm. But then something unexpected happened. The music that started playing on the boom box wasn't hip-hop at all, it was a recording I love, Little Jimmy Scott singing "I'm Afraid the Masquerade Is Over." One of the young guys started miming the performance of the song, with meaningful hand motions and body language. He wasn't lip-syncing, of course, he was wearing a mask. But then, about a minute and a half into the song, where Little Jimmy belts out "I'm afraid the masqueraaaaaaaade is over," drawing the word "masquerade" out for several seconds, the guy pulled off his mask and we could see his mouth wide open. We all gasped. Or at least I did. This guy was lip-belting a Jimmy Scott song, unmasked, in an enclosed subway car! How many billions of viral droplets were spewing from his gaping piehole? Then he surprised us all. He brought his hand to his ear and pulled off what, it turns out, was only a mask of his open mouth. Then we saw a great big smile. Was that a mask too? It was indeed, and he wrapped up his performance in a plain old blue rectangular surgical mask.

Bravo, I thought to myself, as he sang the final words to the song: "And so is love."

When he came around with the hat I showed him a buck's worth of love.

A Statement

I know cloth masks aren't supposed to be as effective as surgical masks or N95, but I wanted to make a statement, so I wore my Kent State mask, featuring a silkscreen of that iconic photo of the shell-shocked young woman leaning over the body of a young man who had just been shot, purchased from the online pandemic pop-up shop of an organization that raises funds for social change initiatives. I had considered one of the other styles, the iconic Vietnam war photo by Eddie Adams of the Viet Cong prisoner of war being shot in the head by a general, the shutter capturing the point of the bullet's impact, but I thought that was just too graphic, that it would upset my fellow pandemic maskers too much, so I chose the more genteel of the two. The Kent State photo was taken by a photojournalism major named John Filo. He won a Pulitzer Prize for it.

I don't think too many people even noticed my mask, though I did see some telling eye action on a few people's upper faces.

I felt somewhat vindicated when I passed four guys stand-ing on the corner, singing harmony behind coordinated blue surgical masks. They were doing "I Only Have Eyes for You," in the Flamingos' arrangement, shoo-bop shoo-bop, but when they saw me they quickly changed their tune. One guy, the lead tenor, sang, "How can you run when you know?" Then the others chimed in, in harmony, "Four dead in Ohio. Four dead in Ohio."

Around the Corner

There was a line, on the street, people standing single file, six feet between them, snaking around the block. I saw the end of the line. I couldn't tell what they were waiting for because, whatever it was, it was around the corner. It must be something pretty good if so many people are waiting, I figured. Everybody in line wore a mask. Some had surgical masks, some had bandanas, some had N95 masks, some had cloth masks in the style of surgical masks, some of which were solid color, most often white or black, and some had prints; my favorite had the Rolling Stones logo, the mouth with the red tongue sticking out of the red lips. I joined the back of the line. I waited. After about five minutes it struck me that the line wasn't moving. I figured I'd give it a little more time. I passed the time listening to a podcast. Another five minutes and still no movement. I called to the person in front of me. "Excuse me," I said, "do you know what we're waiting for?" She gave a shrug. Five more minutes, no change. I'd been waiting in this line for fifteen minutes and it hadn't moved. I turned around and said to the person behind me, "Could you save my place?" I wanted to go around the corner, to take a look, to see what was holding things up. The guy nodded. I got off the line and looked behind me. It stretched the entire length of the block now. My spot was about halfway down the block. I walked the half block to the corner, then turned the corner to see what was going on. Around the corner there was only one person standing, at the head of the line, an elderly man with an N95 mask. The mask covered much of his face, but from his wrinkled brow and white hair I surmised he was elderly. He was just standing there, placid. I spoke to him. "Excuse me, sir," I said, "can you tell me what you're waiting for?"

"Just waiting," he said.

"Just waiting? For what?"

"Just waiting. That's all. I've got nowhere else to be."

I went back around the corner, thanked the guy who was holding my place, and returned to my spot, to wait.

A Chip Off the Old Block

I went to the dermatologist yesterday. It was only my second time on the subway since the lockdown started six months ago. I combined a visit to the dentist, for a check-up and cleaning, in the morning, with an afternoon dermatologist appointment. The subway ride was reassuringly uneventful. There were only a few other people in the car, they all wore masks, and were spread out. I was relieved, as I had approached the ride from Brooklyn to Manhattan with anxiety. I wore a KN95 mask.

I went to the dermatologist because I had this thing on the side of my head, near my right sideburn, that I wanted removed. He had seen it a couple of years ago when it was smaller and flatter, and he told me it was nothing to worry about, but it recently started pushing outward and had become more unsightly, and I was uncomfortable shaving around it, so I wanted it gone. He said it was a keratosis, nothing to worry about, but that if it was bothering me, sure he could he remove it and cauterize the site. He said he'd send a biopsy off to the lab just to make sure.

He said there was no need to remove my mask, that it

wasn't in the way. He gave me an injection, and then did his thing. I didn't feel a thing. Then I heard him say, "Oops!" He turned to the nurse and said, "That was a feisty keratosis. It flew right out and onto the floor. Could you pick it up?" But before the nurse could pick it up, we saw it scamper away, out the door of the examination room. The nurse tried to chase it, but the keratosis was too quick. It was nowhere to be found.

"Nothing to worry about," the doctor said. "Like I said, a biopsy would have been pro forma." Then he cauterized the wound. I felt a little warmth.

"I assume this would feel much hotter if I weren't numbed?" I asked.

"You'd be howling," he said.

He gave me my care instructions and sent me on my way.

Later in the afternoon, I got a call from my bank. "Mr. Cherches?" the representative asked.

"Yes?"

"This is United Bank. We are holding an individual—though I hesitate to use the word—who was trying to withdraw a large sum from your account. We suspected it was an imposter from its appearance. It's a small, brown, irregularly shaped crusty mass, wearing a minuscule surgical mask."

Damn, I thought, my keratosis is trying to commit identity theft! I checked my wallet. My ATM card was gone. The keratosis must have deftly picked my pocket as it flew to the floor.

"That must be the keratosis I had removed earlier today," I said.

"Oh!" the rep said, surprised. "Well, we can freeze your account, destroy the card the er kera..."

"Keratosis."

"That the keratosis tried to use, and send you a new one by overnight."

"That would be great," I said.

"Well, what should we do next? Would you like to press charges? Should I call the police?"

"No," I said, "I don't think that will be necessary. I don't think we can expect any more funny business. You can let it go."

"All right," the rep said. "Is there anything else I can help you with at this time?"

"No, I think we're good."

Damn incorrigible keratosis! The nerve! But it was a part of me once, wasn't it? And it did, after all, wear a mask, and, to tell the truth, that did make me feel rather like a proud papa.

A chip off the old block, my keratosis.

Neighbors

Two old men in N95 masks were having a fistfight in my building's lobby. I could tell who they were by their eyes, their hair, their bodies, the clothes they wore. They were both older than me by 10 or 15 years, mid-to-late-seventies, but I remember when they were younger, as they both were already living here 30 years ago when I first moved in. All these years and I didn't even know their names. I'd nod hello to them, but I can't remember ever having a conversation with either. I'm pretty sure one of them was a widower and one had a wife, a diminutive woman who smiled all the time. I don't remember ever seeing them speaking with each other. Well, they were speaking now, but I wouldn't call it a conversation, more like "You asshole!," pow!, and "You son of a bitch!," pow!

"Hey guys," I said, "calm down. Can't you discuss whatever it is rationally?"

They paid no attention to me. "You moron!," pow!, "You imbecile," pow!

I moved in closer. "Come on guys, break it up."

"You afterbirth!," pow!, "You skid mark on the jockey shorts of eternity!," pow!

"You're not solving anything with violence," I said.

"You pimple on a flea's ass!," pow!, "You smegma-smear on earth's magnetic field!," pow!

I was amazed they were both still standing. Pow! Pow! Pow!

"You over-ripe hunk of gorgonzola!," pow! "You pus-pocket beneath the abscessed tooth of a two-bit centenarian whore!," pow!

They were both bloody all over, red, swollen faces, nosebleeds seeping through the masks, cauliflower ears.

I was starting to worry. Should I come between them, try to break it up?

"You ringworm in a pile of chihuahua shit!," pow!, "You one-way ticket to the worst place on earth!," pow!

Then the little woman showed up, the wife of one of the combatants.

"When are you boys going to grow up?" she said.

They stopped dead in their tracks.

Then she said, "Let's go back upstairs," and to my surprise she got in the elevator with the man who was not her husband.

The other guy had a tear in his eye. He looked at me, sadly, and said, "She left me last month to quarantine with that prick."

And You?

"I recognized you from the eyes," she said. "And the cheekbones."

I hadn't recognized her when she called my name with a question mark at the end. I'm pretty bad with masked faces. "Yes," I answered.

She told me her name. Of course I knew who she was then. We knew each other in college. We were in several creative writing classes together. That was about 45 years ago. I remembered a thing or two about her, details, but I couldn't form a memory of a complete person. A mannerism here or there, maybe a vague sense of the kinds of things she was writing back then.

"I've seen your name," she said. "I see you kept writing."

"Yes," I said, "and you?"

"Nah," she said, a long, drawn out "naaah."

I didn't know what to say next. So I said, "Well, how have you been?"

She said, "I've had my ups and downs."

45 years of ups and downs. I knew better than to ask another question.

"And you?" she asked.

"Oh yeah, me too, ups and downs."

"Now?"

"Generally up," I said. I knew better than to ask, "And you?"

"That's good," she said. There was a pregnant silence. Then she added, "Down."

Research

I don't usually pick up calls from unfamiliar numbers, I let them go to voice mail, but I was expecting a call back from Unemployment to discuss a problem with my claim, so I answered. "Hello?"

I was taken aback by the form of address. "Dr. Cherches?"

"Well," I said, "technically I'm Dr. Cherches, but I never use the title. My doctorate is in American Studies."

"Oh," the man said, "I assumed you were a psychiatrist, or a psychologist or something."

"Why would you assume that?"

"The nature of your research."

"But my scholarly research was about lectures in the 19th century."

"No, I mean your recent research."

"My recent research?"

"Yes, the research you discuss in your article titled 'Mask-Wearing and the Crisis of Self-Identity,' in *The International Journal of Identity Studies.*"

"I wrote no such article."

"Oh, I assumed it was you," the man said. "The bio said, 'Dr. Cherches makes his home in Brooklyn, New York,' and you're the only Peter Cherches I could find in Brooklyn, New York."

"As far as I know I'm the only Peter Cherches in Brooklyn," I said. "*The International Journal of Identity Studies*, you say?"

"Yes."

"I've never heard of it. Which is not to say that questions of identity don't interest me."

"Well," the man said, "I guess there's been some kind of mix-up."

"I suppose," I said. "When did the article come out?"

"It's not out yet. It's in the issue for next spring. I was sent a PDF to review in my journal, *Studies in Identity Studies*. I found your thesis and conclusions very interesting, but I have a few questions."

"It's not my thesis and conclusions," I said.

"Oh," the man said. "I thought you were putting me on about not being the author."

"Why would I put you on?"

"Well," he said, "everything I've read about you concurs that you're the most unreliable of narrators."

"I suppose I used to be," I said. "But wearing a mask in public for the past eight months has made me rethink my narrative gambits."

"That's exactly the part of the article I wanted to ask you about," he said.

Once he told me that I decided to play along, and we had a very pleasant and engaging chat about my article. He did most of the talking and I chimed in with the occasional "Yes," or "Not really," as fit my fancy of the moment.

Dr. Cherches. You know, the title is starting to grow on me after all.

Celebration

The day the victor was called, the streets of my neighborhood were filled with people cheering, honking horns, clanging pots and pans, cowbells, raised arms, fists, V signs, waving at honking cars, waving at each other, hoisting babies, hoisting signs, jubilant, exuberant. Every kind of mask was on display, blue surgical, white N95, bandanas, tubes, cloth masks of every color and pattern. The dancing in the streets was restrained, but everybody seemed to have a bit of a jig in their step.

Conspicuous by its absence, alas, was hugging.

Forgetful

All of a sudden I realized I was out without a mask. Damn. I often forget to put one on, but I almost always catch myself before I leave the building, and I immediately go back upstairs to remedy the situation. But this time I was many blocks away from home. I felt very self-conscious. I'm not carrying my weight in the social contract, I thought. People were looking at me askance. People give me all sorts of looks all the time, but askance not so often. Well, now I was getting askance up the wazoo. I felt like a pariah.

"Pariah!" I heard the mob shout. "Blasphemer of the social contract!" I heard one man in tattered rags say as he paused from self-mortification to make his contempt known to me.

The mob carried torches. They were faceless. They had heads, heads of all colors, with hair atop, but no faces, just smooth, blank skin. But then I noticed that when they screamed at me a little hole where the mouth should be would open up. "Enemy of the people!" they screamed through their little holes. Wait, who were they to scream? None of them were wearing masks.

The maskless, faceless mob surrounded me, taunting me

with their torches, coming ever closer. They're planning to incinerate me, I thought, horrified.

And I woke up with my heart pounding through my chest, breathing with difficulty. Then I realized I was wearing a surgical mask over my nose and mouth. I remembered: I had crashed after a long walk and forgotten to take it off.

I took the mask off. I'll have to throw it away now, I realized, when I noticed the charred edges.

Selfie, 12/15/2020, 11:03 AM

A man sits, at home, in pajama bottoms and a long-sleeve T-shirt, barefoot and unmasked, easy in his easy chair, reading a recent volume of Gilded-Age cultural history, a nostalgic return to a place he once inhabited for his scholarly research, a quarter of a century ago, a favorite genre of nonfiction ever since, *Bitches Brew* the soundtrack of the moment (he usually listens to instrumental music while reading, words get in the way), sipping Assam tea with milk (he had to give up coffee for reflux and found that drinking strong, malty tea in the English way was a substitute he could live with) from a Brooklyn Public Library mug, a gift from his last manager, sun shining through the windows, he's awake and refreshed, having managed seven hours of shuteye, a good take for this chronic insomniac, occasionally setting the book down (actually, his Kindle), thinking back on all those years and all those jobs, the shitty ones and the relatively bearable ones, thinking: This is pretty much how I imagined retirement would be—the pandemic just a footnote to a moment like this.

About the Author

Called "one of the innovators of the short short story" by *Publishers Weekly*, Peter Cherches has lived his creative life in the literary, music, and performance worlds of New York City and beyond for over four decades, as writer, editor, performance artist, singer, and lyricist.

His writing has appeared in scores of magazines, anthologies and websites, including *Transatlantic Review*, *Harper's*, *Bomb*, *North American Review*, *Fiction International*, *Fence*, *Little Star*, *High Times*, *Hambone*, *Semiotext(e)*, and *Poetry 180*. Poet Billy Collins wrote, "To Gödel, Escher, and Bach we might consider adding Peter Cherches." He has published three volumes of short prose with Pelekinesis since 2013: *Lift Your Right Arm*, *Autobiography Without Words*, and *Whistler's Mother's Son*. His previous Bamboo Dart Press chapbook, *Tracks: Memoirs from a Life with Music*, was published in 2021.

Also from Bamboo Dart Press

by Peter Cherches

Tracks: Memoirs from a Life with Music (2021)

In these mini memoirs, Peter Cherches revisits musical experiences, pleasures, and obsessions that have punctuated his life. A singer and lyricist as well as "one of the innovators of the short short story" (*Publishers Weekly*), Cherches writes here from the perspective of a voracious listener for whom music is a constant companion. Whether reminiscing about the joys of musical discovery or paying tribute to musicians who have inspired him, Cherches shares his passions with verve and wit. From an early baptism in Beatlemania, to adolescent encounters with free jazz, to expeditions for local musical treasures around the world, this collection of singles in prose is a testament to the sustaining power of music in our lives.

112 N. Harvard Ave. #65
Claremont, CA 91711

chapbooks@bamboodartpress.com

www.bamboodartpress.com